Sappho: Poems and Fragments

Sappho

Poems and Fragments

Translated, with an Introduction
by
Guy Davenport

Ann Arbor
The University of Michigan Press

Acknowledgment is made of permission to quote
"Fair the Thread" from H.D. Selected Poems,
published by Grove Press, Inc.,
copyright © 1957 by Norman Holmes Pearson

for Mary Ann

In honor of her beauty, her clarity of heart, her love of tree, animal, child, and flower, in memory of her sojourn in Laurelindórinan, in the high meadows, these pages. Vale.

Preface

delicate the weave,
fair the thread:

clear the colours,
apple-leaf green,
ox-heart blood-red:

rare the texture,
woven from wild ram,
sea-bred horned sheep:

the stallion and his mare,
unbridled, with arrow-pattern,
are worked on

the blue cloth

—H.D., "Fair the Thread"

She spoke with Euclidean terseness and authority
of the encounters of the loving heart, the infatu-
ated eye's engagement with flowing hair, suave
bodies, moonlight on flowers. "Mere air, these
words," she is made to say on a fifth-century kylix,
"but delicious to hear." Her imagery is as stark and
patterned as the vase painting of her time: long-
legged horses with dressed manes, marching men,
ships, women in procession to a god's altar. Her
words are simple and piercing in their sincerity, her

lines melodically clean, a music for girls' voices and dancing. Never has poetry been this clear and bright. "Beautiful Sappho," said Socrates.

Somewhere, in the white ruins of Sardis or in a jar still intact in a midden or even on an unexamined shelf, there is perhaps a copy of Sappho's poems complete. Around the mummy of an Alexandrian landlord or Antinoopolitan pastry cook there are, we can guess, for we have found them there before, shrouds of papyrus which were once pages of books on which are written Sappho's smiling conversations with Aphrodite, songs for girls to sing at the moon's altar, and clear evocations of the most graceful young women in ancient literature, their laughter, their bright clothes, their prayers, their girlish loves for men "who looked like gods," for each other, and for older women, their marriages into Lydian families or with the boy down the street— "tall as Ares," as the gracious epithalamies describe him. In Chaucer's girls of the Daisy Cult,

> *As she that is of alle floures flour,*
> *Fulfilled of al vertu and honour,*
> *And evere ilyke·faire, and fressh of hewe;*
> *And I love it, and ever ylike newe,*
> *And evere shal, til that myn herte dye,*

in Francis Jammes' connoisseurship of *jeunes filles en fleur,* in Whistler's and Henry James' white-frocked American girls we can taste something of Sappho's charm and of her vision of adolescent beauty. But Sappho's sure hand at finding the peculiarly feminine flounce that sets her wide-eyed "love of all delicate things" within a sensibility all to itself is so rare that perhaps Gertrude Stein alone among artists of integrity has got anywhere near it, as in "A Sonatina Followed by Another":

> *I caught sight of a splendid Misses. She had handkerchiefs and kisses. She had eyes and yellow shoes she had everything to choose and she chose me. In passing through France she wore a Chinese hat and so did I. In looking at the sun she read a map and so did I. . . . In loving the blue sea she had a pain. And so did I. In loving me she of necessity thought first. And so did I. How prettily we swim. Not in water. Not on land. But in love. How often do we need trees and hills. Not often. And how often do we need mountains. Not very often.*

Even this is protected by a deliberate jauntiness, for all its power to convey. Sappho was infinitely freer, and her gods, a passionate family of high inventiveness in the art of love, urged her on.

But we have only three of her poems whole, together with random lines quoted by rhetoricians and admirers and what archeology has found on a few pottery shards and tattered strips of scrap papyrus, blackened and torn. It has been many centuries since the last-known copy of her poems was worn to shreds by human hands. By the tenth century of our age one could read in an encyclopedia: "Sappho, a harp player from Mytilene in Lesbos . . . . Some write that she was also a lyric poet."

Sappho was a lyric poet of the seventh century before Christ. An older world that, ironically, we know more about, was gone, golden Mycenae, Crete with its labyrinth and bull leapers, Pylos, and all the kingdoms of Homer's epics. That civilization had drifted from the west, away from a trouble we do not yet understand, but which did not touch Attica or the Ionian islands, where the high spirit of the old culture lived on beyond its burnt citadels. The Cretan love of flowers, cunning craftsmanship, and rich needlework, and the Mycenaean splendor of chariots, soldiery, gold, and ships are part of Sappho's heritage. Athens, when she wrote, was a country town with old-fashioned cyclopean battlements. Sparta, not yet rigid with discipline nor fanatically tough and frugal, was what Athens was to become, a city of music and poetry, of games in which boys and girls alike played naked, for modesty's sake. Greek education began there, and thus our own. But Sappho's island, for all the awakening of a new world, dreamed on in antiquity, in touch with the rest of Hellas yet facing the rich and gaudy Lydian empire on the mainland nearby. From here came Sappho's seven-stringed lyre, and the sweetly melancholy mixolydian mode that by one account she gave to Greek music, and her friend the tall Anaktoria.

The seventh century is becoming visible to us. It interests us as the age of Pericles and Plato engaged the Victorians, as Rome of the Republic held the gaze of the eighteenth century. The seventh century's perilous interchange of chaos for order, order for chaos, may remind us of our own. Much was dying, much was being born. Isaiah and Jeremiah, moving in a world much larger than Sappho's, roared at the confusion with fire and vision that we understand all too well. The strenuous flexibility of the rhythms of the next three centuries was beginning. Statues were unfreezing from their Egyptiac stiffness; drawing became graceful, calligraphic, paced like the geometric patterns of weaving and ceramics. Even deep into the oak forests of Europe where the kings rode on reindeer and lived in houses on stilts with dogs half wolf at their feet, drawing— as the rocks of the Camonica Valley show—was returning in the seventh century to a grace and formality that it had not had for a thousand years. This order of the century as it informed its art has become congenial to us through our learning to see Giotto and Altamira, Lascaux and Bulawayo. Within this aesthetic we can place the psychological nakedness of Sappho and her articulation in sunlit space of emotions which we relegate to velleity and aporia.

Spirit, for Sappho, shines from matter; one embraces the two together, inseparable. The world is to be loved. It attracts, we pursue and possess. Its structure contains the goddess Aphrodite who inspires love, and her children Eros and Peitho, who tend to their appointed duties, the lighting of the fire of love in the heart and the seduction of the beloved. These bright framings of animal lust, of loyalty and mutual trust in the breeding season, have taken more dread forms in the history of man, but here the animal is wholly tamed, resplendent in his civilized gentleness.

The Greeks recognized the ambiguous allegiances of adolescence and accommodated them in tensely idealistic and erotic affairs all the more poignant for being brief. Barracks life and athletic training had long before created in the military caste tight friendships among men like Sappho's among women. Maximus of Tyre saw in Sappho's comitatus the beginning of the cohering spirit that Socrates refined into philosophical clarity. "They both appear to me to have practised the same sort of friendship, he of males, she of females, both declaring that they loved many, for they were captivated by all who were beautiful. What Alcibiades, Charmides, and Phaedrus were to him, Gyrinnó, Atthis, and Anaktoria were to her."

These loves were in all probability an affair of the aristocracy; they did not interfere with marriage; they seem to have sprung up among comrades closely engaged in common activity, the army, schools, or, as with Sappho, a cultivated society of high sensitivity. The Greeks were in fact inventing sensibilities which Europe would, in time, transpose wholly to courtship, as when Arnaut Daniel, Sordello, Bertran de Born, and Dante seemed to rediscover romantic love and to incarnate its radiance in a second age of lyric poetry as brilliant, and as far removed from biological process, as Sappho's. *Amabit sapiens,* Lucius Apuleius says in his *Apologia; cupient caeteri.* The educated love; others breed. Apuleius is one of the last authors to understand clearly the old love of adult and adolescent, soldier and recruit, teacher and pupil. "It is not lust but the beauty of innocence that captures lovers," though Sappho knew nothing of the Platonism that colors Apuleius. In fact Sappho puzzled him—her archaic robustness had already begun to look gauche and a bit outrageous. "Her graceful voluptuousness," says this Hellenized Roman, "makes up for the strangeness of her songs." The world could no longer appreciate the impact of a walking, smiling girl upon the heart, as if it were the charioteers of Lydia in full armor charging.

Nor was Sappho's ingenuous Aphrodite as wildly sweet to a world whose religions moved in confusion, eclecticism, and despair. Sappho's Aphrodite is Botticellian and her Graces dance again in his "Primavera." The flower was the pattern for her sense of beauty; she delighted in the frilled leaves of dill and celery—lace upon a slender stalk, so that her girls seem crossbred with flowers. "She wreathes the rose with encomia," Philostratos says of Sappho; rose is symbol of girl; girl, of rose, "roses pale as the fore-arms of Graces, sleeves tucked back at the elbow."

Neither Sappho nor Botticelli separated beauty from the intelligence, of which it is the specious film. Bright eyes, bright mind; balanced walk, balanced nature. The perfect unity of strength and grace in horse, ship, and javelineer underlies her sense of the beautiful, and immediately she demands the enveloping appetence that identifies and completes the beautiful, the untranslatable *imeros*, that yearning which was at once love, sexual longing, adoration, and fascination. Never has a poet been so clear about predilections and attractions. A man should have something of tree, of horse, of a god about him; a girl should have the elegance of the rose and the accomplished Graces. Music, water, air, voices, wine, they must be of a crystal clarity. Where the aesthetic departed from these sharpnesses was in her womanly feeling for the soft and tender: all things colored violet or pink, moonlight, fine cloth, dew, wild flowers, children.

Her Aphrodite laughs. Sexual frenzy was as respectable a passion to her as rapacious selfishness to an American. Few societies have been as afraid of the body as ours, and in the West none has, within history, been as solicitous as the Greek of its beauty. The Egyptian eye first saw dignity and suave elegance in the body, transferring man's millennia of appreciation of the animal's splendor to his own physique. The Egyptian, though wigged in porcelain, braceleted, ringed, and painted, went all but naked; women's clothes kept to the contours of the flesh. It was for the Greek to see the natural growth of the body in full health as a beautiful thing, abhorring all mutilations, scarrings, tattooings, elongations of skull, circumcisions, subtractions of teeth or fingers. The old Aphrodite was fat and long of breast and behind, and the cow was her rich sign. Sappho's Aphrodite was slender, trim of line.

What remains of Sappho, like much of Greek art, is in ruins. But her troubles do not stop there. "The face of Greece," says Nikos Kazantzakis, "is a palimpsest bearing twelve successive inscriptions: Contemporary; the period of 1821; the Turkish yoke; the Frankish sway; the Byzantine; the Roman; the Hellenistic epoch; the Classic; the Dorian middle ages; the Mycenaean; the Aegean; and the Stone Age." He might well have added, since it is constantly before our eyes, the Counterfeit. Its dimensions are astounding. We enter the National Museum in Athens; once we are beyond the great Sounion kouroi and bronze Zeus, or Poseidon, poised to hurl his javelin, we are in a forest of Hellenistic sculpture, Roman copy after Roman copy. Of other classic tokens of Greek art we learn that, like the Winged Victory, what's before us is part real, part conjectural plaster.

At Knossos, deafened by crickets, one sees, surrounded by terebinth, dog rose, and oleander, the ruins of Minos' palace. From here Sappho summoned Aphrodite in a hymn, and here lovely goddesses stage their epiphanies among wild flowers and doves, on wall after wall, in the beautifulest frescoes to have survived antiquity. Here are throne rooms, chapels, long stairs, great jars, cypress pillars rising in the most transparent of light. Did not Daedalos build these walls? A few miles away is a city so old it has had ten names and answers now to three (Candia, Megalo Kastro, Iraklion); its streets have known Hercules, El Greco, Kazantzakis, Dorians, and Nazis, yet beside Knossos it is young.

One looks. These polychrome frescoes, can they have survived from a time that was as remote to Homer as Tiglath-pileser to us? There is no warning posted that they are twentieth-century reconstructions, yet they are, like practically all of the surrounding stage set. The charred originals, themselves pieced together by painted plaster to eke out the design, are in Iraklion. "Eke out" does not adequately describe. Some frescoes are a tenth Knossan, as blackened as Sappho's papyrus fragments, nine-tenths the extrapolation of the reconstructor. And these columns, rooms, stairs, balconies? They are so much the work of Sir Arthur Evans, the Stalin of archeology, that one despairs of knowing Minoan from Victorian architecture. At Phaistos, across the island, nothing has been counterfeited, and all is as flat as time has worn it. "There will always be some," John Bowman says in his *Guide to Crete,* "who feel that Sir Arthur Evans carried his reconstruction rather too far."

Watching the plasterers, painters, and masons at work inside Minos' House of the Double-bladed Ax, building back walls that earthquake had toppled, Dorian fire had burnt, and time had buried, one sees what has happened to too much of Sappho's poetry. I had in my workbook this translation. As Sir Arthur's artists found a bull's ear and horn and have painted a whole bull to be contemplated as an example of Knossan art, I had, not without encouragement from Sappho's nineteenth-century editors, built around the *Sard* of Sardis, taking my moon from the middle of the fragment, what I hoped was a plausible reconstruction. In the closing lines I followed the plasterings over of J. M. Edmonds' *Lyra Graeca,* Edmonds being the Arthur Evans of literature and, as Garry Wills once said, "the only ancient Greek poet to die in the nineteenth century." Thus:

This white moon in its garden of stars
Rises over Sardis in the Lydian night
Where we three in her heart together
Move in grace,

As in those girlish days when you, her goddess,
Sang to adoring ears, before adoring eyes.
Now she walks tall among the wives of Lydia,
Finest of them all,

As brighter among them in her beauty
As when an early moon in the first hour of night
Diminishes with her red hand the brilliant stars
And finds again

Long fields of flowers, the salt sterile sea;
And cool dewfall, unfolding the rose, fills the downs
With parsley and meadows thick with clover bloom.
There, there she walks,

In her country, Atthis, among her people,
And if, holding us in her heart, she calls out in
*   longing*
Across the flower fields, night that has so many ears
Shall hear her cry.

This, as one may see by turning to fragment 43, needed some tuckpointing and a few replaced bricks. Sometimes the entire structure is in ruin, as in this example from the cancelled notebook (and in texts in classrooms where Greek is taught):

Heart, be steady til the anthem come,
For the sovreign Muses would have me sing
Swift crystal sound to hymn the young
Adonis slain.

Instead, you stagger in a trance of lust,
Wild, half human, and by desire disgraced
Fall down before tongue-tying
Aphrodita.

Enticement with seducing eyes
Has poured from her gold two-handled jug
Honied wine to darken deeper your
Forgotten mind.

No such poem of Sappho's exists. The papyrus indeed has words that can be read, here and there, but imagination only can make any sense of them. By giving up the restorer's art, we subtract a great deal of Sappho known to readers of the Loeb Classical Library.

Anthologies made in Alexandrian and Roman times include a fair number of fragile tombstone pieces ascribed to Sappho, such as:

> *Fish-net and oar,*
> *That we remember*
> *His luckless life,*
> *His father Meniskos*
> *Has carved in stone*
> *For Pelagon*
> *The fisherman.*

These, Sappho's severest and best editors, Edgar Lobel and Denys Page, consider to be sentimental ascriptions, and I follow them in omitting the pieces as spurious.

And the fragment that the parrot in Isak Dinesen's story recited in Greek in the Chinese brothel, and which Burns seems to answer in his melancholy

The wan Moon is setting behind the white wave,
> *And Time is setting with me, oh.*

—probably the best known of what we'd thought was Sappho, the poem that might be a woman's or Endymion's voice:

> *The moon has set, and the Pleiades.*
> *It is the middle of the night,*
> *Hour follows hour. I lie alone.*

This is not Sappho, either. It is not written in her dialect.

There is so little of Sappho that the reader with even a little Greek can read the substantial fragments in an afternoon. There are many fine translations of Sappho in English (though none, to my knowledge, that includes all but the utterly hopeless fragments without whole words in them anywhere), and the only excuse for making a new one lies in the richness of her poetry: each translator reflects what he sees, performing not so much a linguistic as a critical act, the closest possible rendering of his appreciation. Many of the fragments are mere words and phrases, but they were once a poem, and, like broken statuary, are strangely articulate in their ruin.

I have generally followed the text as given by Edgar Lobel and Denys Page, *Poetarum Lesbiorum Fragmenta* (Oxford, 1963), and am indebted to Professor Page's *Sappho and Alcaeus* (Oxford, 1959). One can only contemplate with humility the labor that lies behind every printed line of Sappho. A register at the end of the book identifies the Lobel and Page fragment numbers corresponding to mine.

I have separated one two-line fragment back into the discrete lines that some editors place together (*I loved you once, Atthis, long ago / You seemed then to me to be an ungainly little girl*), and I have distributed the index of first lines of poems that appears in the Bibliographical Fragment, Lobel-Page 103. Several times I have given alternate translations, under Roman numerals, since no English version of language so remote in idiom and estranged in culture can be in any sense wholly accurate or final. My starting point was the poems and not the Greek language, my knowledge of which is functional rather than philological. I have followed no strict theory. My intention everywhere has been to suggest the tone of Sappho's words. Had I not accepted as an outer limit to transposing meaning from Greek to English the rule that one must not tamper with grammatical integrity, I could justify, utterly beyond the pale of scholarship, taking the half visible imagery of Fragment 119, for example, and, using the multiple possibilities for what the torn words might have been in their wholeness, making such a poem as:

> *In yellow frock and yellow shawl,*
> *Stole of topaz and peach-flower hat*
> *Knit in your hair like a ring of stars,*
> *In crocus sash and mulberry vest,*
> *Sandals red as amber wine,*
> *You stand in the orchard as*
> *Delicate as the flowering trees.*

This is assuredly not Sappho nor an accepted mode of translation, but it is (or might be, if the guesswork has been lucky) an example of her imagery, much as one displays in a museum ornaments of Mycenaean gold without knowing what they are or how they were articulated in their day. The reading of Sappho is surrounded by passionate dispute in which I am unqualified to join. This translation was made to share my understanding of Sappho with those who care to look.

GUY DAVENPORT

Lexington, Kentucky

Sappho
Poems and Fragments

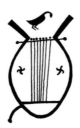

§1

God's wildering daughter deathless Aphródita,
A whittled perplexity your bright abstruse chair,
With heartbreak, lady, and breathlessness
Tame not my heart.

But come down to me, as you came before,
For if ever I cried, and you heard and came,
Come now, of all times, leaving
Your father's golden house

In that chariot pulled by sparrows reined and bitted,
Swift in their flying, a quick blur aquiver,
Beautiful, high. They drew you across steep air
Down to the black earth;

Fast they came, and you behind them, O
Hilarious heart, your face all laughter,
Asking, What troubles you this time, why again
Do you call me down?

Asking, In your wild heart, who now
Must you have? Who is she that persuasion
Fetch her, enlist her, and put her into bounden love?
Sappho, who does you wrong?

If she balks, I promise, soon she'll chase,
If she's turned from gifts, now she'll give them.
And if she does not love you, she will love,
Helpless, she will love.

Come, then, loose me from cruelties.
Give my tethered heart its full desire.
Fulfill, and, come, lock your shield with mine
Throughout the siege.

§2

Come out of Crete
And find me here,
Come to your grove,
Mellow apple trees
And holy altar
Where the sweet smoke
Of libanum is in
Your praise,

Where leaf melody
In the apples
Is a crystal crash,
And the water is cold.
All roses and shadow,
This place, and sleep
Like dusk sifts down
From trembling leaves.

Here horses stand
In flowers and graze.
The wind is glad
And sweet in its moving.
Here, Kypris [   ]
Pour nectar in the golden cups
And mix it deftly with
Our dancing and mortal wine.

§3

I

Nothing can take its place in my mind,
This beauty of girls.

II

Nothing O my girls can stand in my mind
Like your beauty.

§4

I loved you once, Atthis, long ago.

§5

Graces O with wrists like the wild rose,
Chaste and holy daughters, come,
Come among us, daughters of God.

§6

When death has laid you down among his own
And none remember you in all the years to be,
Know, grey among ghosts in that twilight world,
That, offered the roses of Pieria, you refused,
And wander forever in the dark lord Aida's house
Reticent still, with the blind dead, unknown.

§7
[   ] at the temple [   ]
[   ] thickest [   ]
And you O Dika weave with your slender hands
A crown of flowers and dill into those lovely curls,
For she comes first before the serendipitous Graces
Who comes in flowers. The uncrowned they turn
    away.

§8
Spring
Too long
Gongyla

Is there any sign from the oracle
To the girls most of all
Hermes, at least, has entered my dreams

I said, O Lord
Not, I swear, by the blessèd goddess
None can be pleased by that impending

But if ever any longed to die
To see the lotos heavy under dew
On the banks of Acheron

§9
I've fouled the weft, the warp, and the shuttle,
Mother my sweet, bewildered by love, by that boy,
And by the slender Aphrodita.

§10
Why, after so long, should I dream
Of those girlish days?

§11
The little girls
Wove crowns
Of leaves.

§12
Asleep against the breasts of a friend.

§13
The gods [   ] tears [   ]
[   ].

§14

Crying Asia! that famous place,
The messenger came from his dust.
Crying Ektor! the winded runner
Silver with sweat, laughing, Ektor!
Ektor comes from that famous Asia,
From its strange towns with his friends.
They bring home a black-eyed girl
From Theba the high on the Plakia,
The graceful, the young Andrómakha.
They come in the ships on the ocean.
For gifts they bring wrist-chains of gold,
And purple coats and silver jars,
And carved toys incredibly strange,
And things made of ivory.

So the runner said.
                    Quick with astonishment,
Ektor's father shouted for his friends,
And told the coming the city over.
Ilos' boys put wheels to the high carts
And hitched the mules. Wives and girls
Came to stand with Priam's daughters.
Bachelors led the chariot horses;
Charioteers like gods sang commands.

A long parade sings its way from the sea.
The flutes are keen and the drums tight;
Charmed air holds the young girls' songs.
Along the way the people bring them bowls
Of cassia, cups of olibanum and myrrh.
Dancing grandmothers shout the marriage song.
Men and boys march and sing to Páon,
To Apollo of the harp, archer of archers,
And sing that Ektor and Andrómakha
Are like two of the gods together.

§15
Desire has shaken my mind
As wind in the mountain forests
Roars through trees.

§16
You were to me then a shy little girl.

§17
Who is this wild girl with the charm
To get you under her spell? [
[   ] She's always
In a country frock [
Too ignorant to arrange her dress
So that the hem is at the ankle.

§18
With eyes like that, stand still,
Gaze with candor from that beauty,
Bold as friends before each other.

§19
Swallow, swallow,
Pandion's daughter
Of wind and sky,
Why me, why me?

§20

He seems to be a god, that man
Facing you, who leans to be close,
Smiles, and, alert and glad, listens
To your mellow voice

And quickens in love at your laughter.
That stings my breasts, jolts my heart
If I dare the shock of a glance.
I cannot speak,

My tongue sticks to my dry mouth,
Thin fire spreads beneath my skin,
My eyes cannot see and my aching ears
Roar in their labyrinths.

Chill sweat slides down my body,
I shake, I turn greener than grass.
I am neither living nor dead and cry
From the narrow between.

But endure, even this grief of love.

§21
Down from the blue sky
Came Eros taking off his clothes,
His shirt of Phoenician red.

§22
The word went around
          [And]rome[da] was forgotten
Rites and games in their seasons
Sappho O we loved you

To the Queen in Kypros
Tall in our certainty
Daylight was in those eyes
Famous in every ear

Young beyond Acheron.

§23
If only I had drawn such luck from the bowl
O Aphrodita crowned with golden leaves.

§24

[   ]
[   ] that labor [   ]
[   ] a face to remember in wonder [
[   ]

[   ] to sing [   ]
[   ] a storm wind [   ]
[   ] and no pain [   ]
[   ]

[   ] I urge [   ]
Gongyla [   ] harp
[   ] whose longing again
Hovers on wings

Around your loveliness. For when she sees
The long pleats of your dress in their moving
She catches her breath at the beauty,
And I laugh for joy.

Goddess born from the sea at Kypros
Thus I pray [   ]
That [   ]
I long [   ].

§25
I
A company of horsemen or of infantry
Or a fleet of ships, some say,
Is the black earth's finest sight,
But to me it is what you love.

This can be understood in its round truth
By all, clearly, for she who in her beauty
Surpassed all mankind, Elena, left her husband,
The best of men,

And sailed to Troia, mindless of her daughter,
And of her parents whom she loved.
But [   ]
[   ] led her astray.

[   ]
[   ] lightness in her heart [   ]
That I remember Anaktoria now
So far away.

I would rather see the fetching way she walks
And the smiling brightness of her eyes
Than the chariots and charioteers of Lydia
In full armor charging.

[   ] cannot become
[   ] man [   ] approach with sacrifice and
    pray
[   ]
[   ].

II

Handsome horses O shiver and admire,
Long ships and symmetries of archers,
But black earth's fine sight for me
Is her I love.

Heart's hunger all can understand.
Did not she up and leave the best of men,
Helen that beautifulest of womankind?
[   ]

And forgot her kin and forgot her children
To follow however far into whatever luck
The wild hitherward of her headlong heart
[   ]

[   ]
[   ]
Anaktoria so far away, remember me,
Remember me, who had rather

Hear the melody of your walking
And see the torch-flare of your smile
Than the long battle-line of Lydia's charioteers,
Round shields and helmets.

§26
And there, when they had stirred
The magic liquor in the jug,
And Ermais, in each held out cup
Had poured from a leather bottle
Every god his ambrosia,
Each tipped some out, for piety,
And rang his cup against another,
That all bright and noble things
Come to our new kinsman.

§27
Sweetpeas flowered golden
All over the marsh.

§28
Too much is enough
Of that girl Gorgo.

§29
Air
Bound
Cu[p
Mus[lin
Forth[with
Of sleep
[*five lines
  indecipherable*]
Beautiful
Fluttering
[   ] ivory
Cl[asp.

§30
They wore red yarn to bind their hair,
Our girls when they were young,
This, or no finery at all.

That, to be grand [
But those labyrinthine curls of yours,
Yellower than [

Great overhanging hat of leaves
And the fattest of flowers,
With a snug and perfect snood

Embroidered, Persian, and from Sardis,
That [   ] city
[   ]

And, Kleïs, I do not have for you
That rich embroidered snood
That you want, but in Mytilena [

[   ]
Girls [   ] to have [
If the embroidered

These Kleanaktida [
You flee [
These memories. Know that our name is gone.

§31
Bride with beautiful feet.

§32
Though you are my lover,
Take for wife a younger woman;
Find a newer bed to live in,
I could not bear to be the older.

§33
Dusk and western star,
You gather
What glittering sunrise
Scattered far,
The ewe to fold,
Kid and nanny home,
But the daughter
You send wandering
From her mother.

[   ]
Hesperos, most beautiful
Of stars.

§34
And your boy's beauty,
What else is so trim, so lithe,
Impetuous follower?
Straight slender trees
Have that balance.

§35
[   ]
silent, still
the holy goatskin wearing
Kytherean, I am praying
she who owns my mind
hear my prayers, so high
she who has left me behind
against me green
harsh [

§36
Never, Irana, have I met anybody
More bothersome than you.

§37
I
With quickened heart they hovered,
Fluttered, and lit with folding wings,
The doves. My heart is cold.

II
Their wings fold down,
My heart grows chill.

§38
Loving girls more than Gello.

§39

She had others at Kytherea to nurse her,
But Peitho, they say, is the daughter of Aphrodita
[   ]
A gift for honor [
And Gyrinno [
[   ]
But never say that [
Beautifully you speak [
[   ]
The west wind blows upon me
[   ]
Sliding across the air
            on wings spread wide
[   ]
She writes these matters to Andromeda.

§40

She was like that sweetest apple
That ripened highest on the tree,
That the harvesters couldn't reach,
And pretended they forgot.
[   ]
Like the mountain hyacinth trod underfoot
By shepherd men, its flower purple on the ground.

§41
Wrapped up in rich shaggy wool.

§42
[   ] of Eros, anxious [   ]
[   ]
[   ] I admire, I gaze at you [   ]
[   ] Ermiona herself, and like her
[   ] you are as blonde as Elena,
[Decorous, suave].
[   ] to mortal women, but know this
[   ] me [   ] all solicitude
[   ] but
[   ]
[   ] dew of the riverside gleaming
[   ]
[   ] to make it last all night long.

§43
[   ] Sard [is   ]
How many times she must remember us here
Where once [   ] we [   ]
She had divinity in her.

Her dancing, of all, was your enchantment.
And now she moves among the Lydian ladies
As when the sun has set and the stars come out
And the rose red moon

Lifts into the midst of their pale brightness.
Her light is everywhere, on the salt-bitter sea,
On fields thick and rich with flowers
And beautiful under dew,

On roses, tangled parsley, and the honey-headed
        clover.
Her light is everywhere, remembering
Atthis in her young sweetness, desiring her
With tender, heavy heart.

There, in that far place, that we come [
Knows not [   ] many
Hears [   ] the between
[   ].

They are not mine, the deerhide shoes of Asia,
That body to hold, with its goddess's beauty
To have against [
[   ].

Soft [   ] Eros
And [   ] Aphrodita
[   ] nectar poured into
Golden [   ].

[   ] enticement with her hands
[
[
[   ].

[   ] in the month of Geraistios
[   ] lovers
[   ] never
[   ] I shall come.

§44
They gave me honor,
The gift of their skill.

§45
Her shoes were leather and from Asia,
Rich Lydian patterns across the toes.

§46
[   ] Mika
[   ] I shall not let you
You have taken Penthilea for your sweetheart,
Treating me with less than kindness
[   ] and a song, sweet
[   ] with low, gentle voice
[   ] crystal clarity in that song
[   ] dewfall upon the world.

§47
Came husband,
        mischief,
]ing bri[ght]

§48
Don't stir
The trash.

§49
Where do the butler's big feet go?
Fourteen yards from heel to toe!
Five red oxen gladly died,
Ten frantic cobblers stitched the hide,
That stylish slippers trim and neat
Besplendor those important feet.

§50
High in the chariot,
As when the mastersinger of Lesbos
Against all the outlanders.

§51
Violet-breasted daughter of Kronos.

§52
As once in Crete,
A round dance of girls
In that antique time.

§53
She taught the champion runner,
Hero of Gyara.

§54
Arkheanassa and Gorgo
Sleep together as married folk,
Wherefore she is called her wife.
And Pleistodiké, she was her wife
In between Gongyla and Gorgo.
They've given themselves a name
Together and [   ] Pleistodiké
[   ] shall be known as
[   ].

§55
With that island-born
Holiness of Kypros
I talked; she talked,
And all in a dream.

§56
Now that Andromeda has her fair reply
[   ]
Psappho, why Aphrodita of so many pleasures?

§57
All yellow gold and like a daughter,
A flower, that girl, with a flower's beauty,
And, Kleïs, not for all the girls in Lydia,
My word of honor on our friendship,
Nor for all the Mytilenian virgins,
Would I leave her.

§58
[   ]
For the sake of the old
[   ]
Voice [   ]
Before [   ].

§59
And then [   ]
Not even one [   ]
And now [   ]
Nor wishes [   ]
Mnasidika is more beautiful of body
Than the svelte Gyrinno.

§60
Rose
[   ]
Speak
[   ]
Yearning
[   ]
Sweat.

§61

I
brightness and
[   ]
with luck in the outcome
overcomes
black
[   ]
sailors
high winds
and on shore
[   ]
sails
the cargo
[   ]
streaming, many
[   ]
work
of the land
[   ].

II
Pray now the women
          at Demeter's altar
Prophecies, songs,
          brightness and
[   ]
Fortunate and well-bred together
          crushes, crashes
These black ships
Haul in and batten, the sailors,
High seas, heavy weather, gales,
Reefs and land off port
[   ]
          far more than
                    the cargo shifting
                    oarlocks awash, waves
[   ]
     many that
[   ]
          desperation,
     land
[   ].

§62
Aphrodita
delightful words
may throw
holding
sits
[   ]
seafoam.

§63
For Aphrodita, this purple handkerchief
To wear on her head against the heat,
An honored gift from Phokaia.

§64
O there are no others like her,
Not in these times, lover.

§65
I
Percussion, salt and honey,
A quivering in the thighs;
He shakes me all over again,
Eros who cannot be thrown,
Who stalks on all fours
Like a beast.

II
Eros makes me shiver again
Strengthless in the knees,
Eros gall and honey,
Snake-sly, invincible.

§66
You hate me who loves you, Atthis,
And flutter around Andromeda.

§67
O Pollyanna
Polyanaktidas,
Goodbye, goodbye.

§68
Golden goblets with knucklebone stems.

§69
I am Aphrodita of the shifting eyes.
My servants are Eros and you, my Sappho.

§70
The scholar Aristides, pondering
material and spiritual wealth,
recalls that Sappho in a poem said:

The Muses have made me happy
And worthy of the world's envy,
So that even beyond death
I shall be remembered.

§71
[   ] downward my tears [   ]
Let trouble come to sting the whipper
And a high wind blow him away.

§72
And I yearn
And I hunt.

§73

The stars around the moon in her beauty
Dim their bright patterns of fire
When her light is full upon the world.

*The Emperor Julian, mentioning Sappho in a letter,
seems to have remembered these lines as:*

When the moon is silver
She hides the stars around her
From our sight.

§74

Daughter of kings
The sons of kings,
Hail!

§75

I

The night is long but girls will sing
Songs all night outside your door
To keep you from her violet softness.

Leave her alone! Go back to your friends,
Or all night long, like nightingales,
We shall stay awake and sing.

II

Leave your siege of her violet softness.
The night is long but we shall sing
Epithalamia outside your door.

Call to your bachelor friends to come.
All night long, like the nightingale,
We shall stay awake and sing.

§76

For even then, when you were a little girl,
Come on! you said, *let's sing to your lyre*
[   ]
[   ] you were never far from me,
A wonder of gracefulness.

And now we walk to a wedding,
Beautifully you [
[   ] send the girls quickly
[   ] might have
[   ] the road to high Olympos
[   ] men [   ].

§77
[   ] frequent- [   ]
[   ] because those I do the most for
Hurt me the worst
[   ] idle [   ]
[   ] on the knees [   ]
[   ]
[   ]
               ] you, I am willing [
               ] suffering [
               ] and I, for myself [
This I knew something about [
[   ] for them [

§78

Before my lying heart could speak for life
I longed for death. Misery the size of terror
Was in her tears when we unclasped forever.
Sappho! she cried,

That I could stay! Joy goes with you, I said,
Remember what has been, the rose-and violet
     crowns
I wove into your hair when we stood so close
     together,
Heart against heart,

The garlands I plaited of flower with flower
Around your graceful neck, the oils of spices
As precious as for a queen [
[   ].

Deep in the cushions on that softest bed
Where, free in desire [
[   ] tender lovers
[   ].

None [   ] holy, and no [
There was, that we were apart from [
No sacred grove [
[   ].

§79
First news of springtime,
The lovesong of the nightingale.

§80
I have neither the honey nor the bee.

§81
Haughtier than a horse.

§82
And let her find you, Kyprian, bitterer still,
To keep her loud tongue from saying ever
That Eros hot and flustering came to Dorikha
A second time.

§83
[   ]
around
you, Atthis
cloud-
[   ]

§84
of Dorikha
    called, and no
[   ]
to reach for, arrogance of heart
to be half asleep with love
[   ]

§85
heart
altogether
I can
[   ]
may be for me
throws back the light
[hand]some face
[   ]
caressed
[   ]

§86
staying
in the burnt offering
her, holding the finest

and she, walking
for we saw
of the work
[   ]
and back again
[   ]
to say this

§87
[   ]
Graces
[   ]
you, at least
[   ].

§88
shall give
no matter what
the beautiful and the splendid
you may grieve
my disgrace
rising, on
were you pained
not this way
is [she] inclined
nor yet
                    I understand
                    the worst man of all
                    [   ]
                    to the others
                    the mind
                    luck-
[   ].

§89
[   ]
not even
lovely
[   ]
flower
longing
pleased
[   ].

§90
Someone, I'm bold to say,
Will remember us
In time hereafter.

§91
Wealth without moral splendor
Makes a dangerous neighbor;
But join the two together:
There is no higher fortune.

§92
Sometimes she closed her eyes
All night long.

§93
Far more melodious than the harp,
More golden than gold.

§94
Lady Dawn.

§95
When fury rages in the breast,
Watch that reiterating tongue.

§96
Softer than a fine dress.

§97
These pleasures now, my constant girls,
I shall sing in splendid songs.

§98
While they kept watch around her
[   ] the bridegrooms
[   ] lords of the town.

§99
To whose eyes?

§100
Eros weaver of myths,
Eros sweet and bitter,
Eros bringer of pain.

§101

[   ] slick with slime [   ]
[   ] Polyanaktidas to satiety [   ]
[   ] shoots forward [   ]
Playing such music upon these strings
Wearing a phallus of leather [   ]
Such a thing as this [   ] enviously
[   ] twirls quivering masterfully
[   ] and has for odor
[   ] hollow [   ]
[   ]
[   ] mysteries, orgies
[   ] leaving
[   ] an oracle
[   ] comes [   ]
[   ]
[com]panions
[mys]teries
[   ]
[   ]
[   ] sister
So [   ]
[   ] wishes [   ]
Displays again Polyanaktidas [   ]
This randy madness I joyfully proclaim.

[   ]
Her [
Man [
And see[ms
These girls al[l
Topmost [
Wanders [
[   ] these [
[   ]
Partner [
Own cousin [
Elbows [
Laughing away [
This [
The [
Cries O [
Blood [
Sharp [
[   ]
[   ]
Well [
Shall please again [
And from [
O girls [
[   ].

§102

Raise the ridge-pole higher, higher,
O marriage night O binding god
Carpenters! Make the roof-tree taller,
O marriage night O binding god
He comes, the husband, and walks like Ares,
O marriage night O binding god
He's taller by far than a tall man,
O marriage night O binding god.

§103
Mermaids and you brine-born on the Kypros sand,
Bring back my brother over your sea unhurt,
That his wandering heart have for its own
Its real desire.

Wash off all that wrong upon his head;
Make him a brightness to those who love him
[   ] to his enemies a distress,
and let none hereafter [

Let him be willing to do honor to his sister
[   ] and the miserable
        sorrows
[   ] grieving as we did
        before
[   ]

[   ] hearing the [   ] of the millet,
Townspeople murmuring in the marketplace
[   ] and again no
[   ]

[   ]
[   ] and you, Kyprian [   ]
[   ] put away the evil [   ]
[   ].

§104
Kyprian and sea-daughters of Nereos,
Grant to my brother that he come here
Unharmed, and that all the wishes in his heart
Come to be fulfilled,

Let him be washed clean before the gods,
That he be a delight to all who love him.

§105
Near me [
Lady Era [
Their praying, the princes of Atreos [
The kings [

Brought to its end [
From the beginning around [
At a loss for their passage here [
They could not.

Till you and Zeus [
And of Thyona the love[ly
And now [
In the manner of old [

The pure and chaste [
Girls [
Around [

[   ].

§106

I

Stand beside me, worshipped Hera, strange in a
     dream,
Ghost or visitation but in a shape all grace,
Sudden as before the famous Mycenaean kings
When they cried out

At the awful end of pulling Troy to the ground,
Their ships turned homeward down the rapid
     Skamander,
And knew that lest you guide them they were
     luckless,
And prayed your love,

And called to strongest Zeus and Thyona's son
The cherished. Like them, lady queen, I ask
To return to my country, homecoming with your
Benediction,

That among the virgins of Mytilene, as before,
I perform the chaste and holy rites in splendor,
And teach the dances and make songs for the holy
     days.
O bring me home.

II

Before me, Potni' Era, appear to mortal eyes,
Clear of body, beautiful, bright,
As when the far-sung Atridaean princes
Stood, as I, in prayer:

Who fought so hard at Ilion's wall,
Wandered so long over all the sea,
Lost, after so much labor and death,
Helpless to return

Until they cried to you, to Zeus Antiaos,
And to Thyona's darling son, their prayer.
Treat me now in those ancient ways,
Bring grace upon me.

The chaste [
Virgins [
Around [
[   ].

§107

Whether you are at Kypros and Paphos
Or at Panormos.

§108

You make me hot.

§109

I gave you a white goat.

§110

[   ]
                    beautiful
                    peace become havoc
                    weariness of heart
                    sits down against
                    but up, O friends
                    for day is nigh

[   ]

§111

Until all of you are willing.

§112

You have come, and done,
And I was waiting for you
To temper the red desire
That burned my heart.

§113

Beauty is for the eyes and fades in a while,
But goodness is a beauty that lasts forever.

§114
I don't know which way I'm running.
My mind is part this way, part that.

§115
    ] come forward, tell [

§116
Bridegroom, exult! Just as you prayed,
The rites are done and you are married.
The girl, just as you prayed, is yours.
[   ]
All gracefulness your body and your eyes
[   ]
Softly Eros rises in your longing face
[   ]
Aphrodita has honored you above all.

§117
Wet handkerchief.

§118
ALKAIOS
I have something I'm willing to tell you,
But bashfulness holds me back.

SAPPHO
If your heart is for the noble and beautiful
And your tongue is free of all things ugly,
Reticence need not lower your eyes:
Speak out whatever is fitting and right.

§119
[
[
[Her] shirt
Yel[low]
[Her] petticoat
And splendor
Radiant yellow
[Her] red dress
Robes the color of peaches
Peach-flower crowns
Pretty eyes
Phrygian
Red
Carpet
[
P[

§120
Dawn with small golden feet.

§121
Parthenia, parthenia,
poi me lipois' apoikhe?
Girlhood O girlhood,
Lost of a sudden,
Where have you gone?

Ouketi exo
pros se
ouket' exo,
Nowhere, bride my darling,
nowhere near you.

§122
]him[
[   ]
]becomes[

§123
Black dreams of such virulence[
That sleep's sweetness[
And terrible grief[
This place is religious[
Happiness, no, and hope neither[
And I indeed am so[
Delightful the games[
And I[
This[

§124
There are none like her,
And none will ever see the light of the sun,
None hereafter will have that mastery.

Or, to accommodate another meaning of sophia:

I cannot believe there is any girl
Under the sun, or shall be to come,
With an intelligence like hers.

§125
] curls [   ] placing the lyre.

§126
] bridegroom, for your tiresome bachelor friends

§127

[   ]
        toward
[
        should you be willing
        few
        to be borne
        any
        regard that pleasure
        you know and
        have forgotten but grief
[
        if any speak
        for I also
        no longer than to the day after tomorrow
        to be loved
        love, I say, will become strong
[
        and grievous
        sharp
[
        and know this
        whoever you
        will love
[
[
        of the arrows
[   ].

§128
Clear keen song.

§129
A phrase remembered by Aristides
when he was talking about the clear
light of Smyrna:

Brightness that strikes the eyes

§130
O beautiful, O graceful

§131
When songs from the heart.

§132
When she, the round moon, rose,
They stood in a ring around her altar.

§133
To Gyrinno.

§134
I put here, my lazy girl, this soft cushion,
And if, with your blouse off, in your soft arms.

§135
Pure and holy Graces and Muses who live at Pieria

§136
Place there the nature of the violet breasted.

§137
Slender Graces and Muses with beautiful hair,
Come hither, come now.

§138
He is dying, Kytherea,
The young Adonis,
What can we put around him?

Beat your breasts, girls,
Tear your dresses.

§139
[   ]
all
and the other
[   ]

§140
More valuable than gold.

§141
fragrant-
[*five lines indecipherable*]
walk
thus see
[   ]
lady
golden-
[   ]
[   ]
[   ].

§142
Those discords,
I don't think,
Will reach the sky.

§143
Seven ways in terror,
        the laurel tree,
                a forest all of pine,
The empty,
And these
                the wayfarer
As the mouse, silent, hidden,
O girlish heart,
        a mind so calm that
Comes with kisses and open arms
Seven
        her beauty
Is.

§144
[   ]
pretty
Artemis
[   ]

§145
You too, Kalliopa,
Yourself.

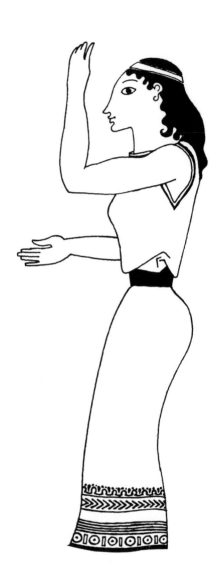

§146

        ] called you
      ] filled your mouth with plenty
      ] girls, fine gifts
    ] lovesong, the keen-toned harp
    ] an old woman's flesh
    ] hair that used to be black
    ] knees will not hold
    ] stand like dappled fawns
       ] but what could I do?
    ] no longer able to begin again
      ] rosy-armed Dawn
        ] bearing to the ends of the earth
         ] nevertheless seized
          ] the cherished wife
         ] withering is common to all
       ] may that girl come and be my lover
I have loved all graceful things [   ] and this
Eros has given me, beauty and the light of the sun.

§147
I am willing.

§148
Once upon a time, the story goes,
Leda found a hyacinthine egg.

§149
Tenderer than the rose.

§150
A coronet of celery.

§151
To die is evil.
The gods think so,
Else they would die.

§152
Hail, bride!
Hail, honored bridegroom!
Long life!

§153
More harmonious than lyres.

§154
[   ]
loves
[   ].

§155
] as it happens
] wishes, being childless still
] I see the fulfilment
] I summoned
] all of a sudden against my heart
] as much as you wish it to come about
] to struggle against me
] is voluptuous in her enticement
] but you know well

§156
It is not fitting to mourn the dead
In a house where the Muses are served.
Let us have no mourning here.

§157
Muses, come down again,
Leaving that golden [

§158
Weaker than water

§159
[   ]
[   ]
the festival
[   ]

§160
Eros, child of Gea and Ouranos.

§161
Whiter than milk.

§162
The goddess Persuasion,
Daughter of Aphrodita.

§163
Medeia.

§164
Lato and Nioba were very loving friends.

§165
All colors tangled together.

§166
We shall give, Father said.

§167
me away from them
and we became
like the gods
against the gods
Andromeda
[   ]
no longer unstained
Tyndarides
with grace
honest no more with
the great palaces
[   ]
the doors
in a fury
the guard corporal
wrestling
[   ]

§168
And night's black sleep upon the eyes.

§169
Your darling.

§170
With the bride that happy,
Let the bridegroom rejoice.

§171
Of the Muses.

§172
Whiter by far than an egg.

§173
[   ] I
[   ]
[   ]
I hold the quince [
    ] of the little girls.

§174
The island Aiga.

§175
Barbitos. Baromos. Barmos.

§176
As good natured as a little girl,
I don't snap and pout and rage.

§177
The dress.

§178
[   ]
      here
[   ]
      again
[   ]

§179
She calls her daughter.

§180
A girl picking a flower just opened.

§181
above
you shall remember
in our girlhood
we made
for and
the town-
[*several lines gone*]
facing
[   ]
endurance
man
[   ]
all
[*more lines gone*]
fine small voice
[   ]

§182
Handbag.

§183
Falling downward.

§184
Ektor.

§185
All that's lo[ved]
Tell
Tongue
Mythology
And to men
Larger-

§186
And this [
Grief from the divine powers [

Surely [   ] did not love [
And now because [

And the responsibility [
Nor many [

§187
Became [
For no [

§188
Gentle of voice.

Or, considering
the scribe's spelling:

With honey in her words.

§189
[   ]
chtho[nic   ]
[   ]

§190
Vines trellised on poles.

§191
I might lead.

§192
[   ]
and I go
[   ]
and surely you failed
harmony
the dance
[   ]

§193
That man seems to her.

§194
Trench for watering the garden.

§195
Danger.

§196
Wise in many things.

§197
Soda.

§198
Without guile.

§199
I wish to go.

§200
[   ]
anointing
[   ]
forgetfulness
[   ]
bedroom

§201
Ford at the river.

§202
[   ]
peers
[   ]
of children
[   ]
[*several*
  indecipherable
  lines]
gods
shameful
[   ]

§203
O Adonis!

§204
Dawn.

§205
The girl with the pleasing voice.

§206
You have begun to forget me [
        ] or do you love some other?

§207
Just when dawn in her golden sandals.

§208
beforehand
to carry
and willing
Arkheanassa
whenever in dreams
the softball umpire
fell in love
·
[   ]
receive
[   ]
·
[   ]
upon
speech[less
[   ]
·
[   ]
heard
Kran[n]iades
girls
[   ]

§209

     done, cast
     compassion
     trembling
     [   ]
     old age and wrinkles so soon
     wanders around
     flies in pursuit
     [   ]
     of the noble
     she, taking
     sang to us
The violet-breasted
     [   ]
     most of all
     the wandering

§210

Lead off, my lyre,
And we shall sing together.

Notes

The numbers in brackets refer to Edgar Lobel and Denys Page,
Poetarum Lesbiorum Fragmenta *(Oxford University Press,*
1963). The initial number refers to the fragment.

1. [1] *Poikilothronos,* "a cunningly wrought chair," may
mean a chair piled full of richly embroidered cushions, for
poikilos seems most often to describe intricately patterned
needlework, or patchwork of some sort, involving many
colors. But Sappho has many cushions in her poems and
would have put them here if she thought Aphrodite had
them on her throne. I take the fancy chair from the
Linear B furniture lists, where we find "one table, of
ebony, with ivory supports, splay-legged, decorated with
shell pattern," and "one chair with golden birds on the
back and a footstool inlaid with ivory rosettes," and "one
chair, of crystal, inlaid with cyanus, tin, and gold . . ."
Leonard B. Palmer, *Mycenaeans and Minoans: Aegean*
Prehistory in the Light of the Linear B Tablets (New
York: Alfred A. Knopf, 1963), p. 152.
that persuasion / fetch her: Gods, abstract concepts, and
states of mind are not easily distinguishable in the Greek
mind; Sappho may mean the goddess Persuasion, Peitho,
daughter of Aphrodite. Sappho prefers her to her male
counterpart Eros.
enlist her . . . shield: the tight friendships of Sappho
and her friends with adolescent girls seem from the military imagery to suggest a conscious parallel with that
between men and boys in the Greek armies.

2. [2] From a pottery shard. Kypris is Aphrodite.

3. [41].

4. [49, line 1].

5. [53].

6. [55]. *Aida:* Hades. Written, seemingly, to a stand-offish girl. Thomas Hardy translates this in a poem called *Achtung.*

7. [81]. *Dill:* the aromatic herb *(Anethum graveolens),* the same as we use for pickling. Its leaves, together with those of celery, were woven into garlands and worn around the head.

8. [95]. The opening lines probably mean: "I lifted up / [ ] / Gongyla," but the misreading, if misreading it be, is by this time too resonant to change, and there's nothing crucial in them to our understanding of the fragment.

   Hermes: Sappho sang Ermais.

9. [102].

10. [107].

11. [125].

12. [126].

13. [139].

14. [44]. The marriage of Hector and Andromache. The meter and dialect are epic. The opening lines are in ruin, but Kypris is mentioned, and the herald's name seems to be Idaos.

15. [47].

16. [49, line 2].

17. [57].

18. [138].

19. [135].

20. [31].

21. [54].

22. [65]. A papyrus blackened at the top and torn down the right side.

23. [33].

24. [22].

25. [16]. *Elena:* Helen.

26. [141]. *magic liquor:* nectar. *There* is emphatic, and was a way of designating the dwelling of the gods.

27. [143].

28. [144]. Gorgo is probably a nickname, an affectionate insult among close friends. Mary Barnard suggests the school-girlish *Monkeyface* as an equivalent.

29. [97]. Only the extreme left side is readable.

30. [98]. Kleïs was Sappho's mother or daughter. This song seems to have been written during a political exile; the Kleanaktides were the hostile faction in power in Lesbos.

31. [103.5].

32. [121].

33. [104].

34. [115]. For once I take *gambros* (bridegroom, husband, son-in-law, kinsman) in its sense of *suitor*.

35. [86]. Holy goatskin: the aegis.

36. [91].

37. [42].

38. [178].

39. [90]. Peitho: the goddess Persuasion or Enticement.

40. [105].

41. [100].

42. [23]. Ermiona: Hermione. Elena: Helen.

43. [96].

44. [32]. The Muses gave the honor.

45. [39].

46. [71].

47. [69].

48. [145].

49. [110]. The butler guards the bridal chamber; the song would seem to be for the shivaree that went on all night after a wedding.

50. [106].
51. [103, line 6]. Aphrodite.
52. [Incert. 16].
53. [Incert. 11].
54. [213].
55. [134].
56. [133].
57. [132].
58. [85].
59. [82].
60. [74].
61. [20]. Part of the right-hand half of a poem. My opening for version II is guesswork, based on what may be the word for an altar to Demeter.
62. [73].
63. [101]. The Greek contains scribe's errors and is not at all clear.
64. [113].
65. [130].
66. [131].
67. [155]. A satiric version of 74.
68. [192].
69. [159].
70. [193].
71. [37].
72. [36].
73. [34].
74. [155]. Same as 67, allowing for the possibility of a serious tribute, and reading *polyanaktidas* as an epithet rather than a girl's name.
75. [30]. A wedding-night song.
76. [27].
77. [26].

78. [94]. The opening line is: *I honestly wish to die.*

79. [136]. Ben Jonson was aware of this fragment and quotes it in *The Sad Shepherd* (II.vi.85-86) as "the deare, good Angell of the Spring, / The Nightingale."

80. [146]. Hilda Doolittle gives an imaginative extension of this fragment in her poem Fragment 113, *Selected Poems* (New York, 1957), pp. 36-37.

81. [156].

82. [15].

83. [8].

84. [7]. The last line is a guess.

85. [4].

86. [19].

87. [77].

88. [3].

89. [78].

90. [147].

91. [148].

92. [149].

93. [156].

94. [157].

95. [158].

96. [156].

97. [160].

98. [161].

99. [162].

100. [172 + 188].

101. [99].

102. [111].

103. [5].

104. [5]. Another version.

105. [17].

106. [17]. Another version, following reconstructions (Edmonds, Page) that seem plausible.

107. [35]. Places sacred to Aphrodite.

108. [38].

109. [40]. The Greek is not clear and may be a miscopying.

110. [43].

111. [45].

112. [48]. Literally, "cool the burning desire in my heart."

113. [50]. The sense is more blatantly Greek than I have been able to suggest: "He who is beautiful is beautiful only as long as he's beautiful to the eyes, but he who is also good, will be beautiful all his life."

114. [51].

115. [103, line 4].

116. [112]. After the first three lines it would seem that the song turns its attention to the bride.

117. [119].

118. [128]. Alkaios, Sappho's contemporary and fellow poet.

119. [92].

120. [103, line 13].

121. [114].

122. [79].

123. [63].

124. [56]. *Sophia:* mastery of a skill, intelligence, wisdom.

125. [103, line 12].

126. [103, line 11].

127. [88].

128. [103, line 10].

129. [196].

130. [108].

131. [103, line 9].

132. [154].

133. [29].

134. [46]. The Greek is probably miscopied, filled with word play and puns.

135. [103, line 8].

136. [103, line 7]. I.e., the nature of Aphrodite.
137. [128].
138. [140].
139. [80].
140. [156].
141. [6].
142. [52]. The Greek is not clear.
143. [62].
144. [84].
145. [124].
146. [58]. The myth of Tithonos is probably alluded to in the lines about Dawn.
147. [76].
148. [166].
149. [156].
150. [191].
151. [201]. Quoted by Aristotle.
152. [116].
153. [156].
154. [59].
155. [60].
156. [150].
157. [127].
158. [156].
159. [9].
160. [198]. Gea, the earth, Ouranos, the sky.
161. [156].
162. [200]. The goddess Peitho, Persuasion.
163. [186].
164. [142].
165. [152]. A description of Jason's coat.
166. [109].
167. [68].Torn down both sides.
168. [151].

169. [163].
170. [117].
171. [187].
172. [167].
173. [93].
174. [170].
175. [176]. The names of three kinds of lyre.
176. [120].
177. [177].
178. [83].
179. [164].
180. [122].
181. [24]. Torn down both sides.
182. [179].
183. [183].
184. [180]. Hector.
185. [18]. Right-hand side missing.
186. [67].
187. [61].
188. [185].
189. [28].
190. [173].
191. [169].
192. [70].
193. [165].
194. [174].
195. [184].
196. [190].
197. [189].
198. [171]. Or: without evil intent.
199. [182].
200. [25].
201. [181].

202. [64].
203. [168].
204. [175].
205. [153].
206. [129]. "Some other of all mankind," says the Greek.
207. [123].
208. [214]. Four fragments that seem to belong together.
209. [21].
210. [118].